T0358146

THE HULK

The Hulk

BY SIMON ROBB

Published by Post Taste Media and Publishing Pty Ltd
PO Box 160 Bulahdelah NSW 2423 Australia
ABN 63 094 087 288
info@posttaste.com
www.posttaste.com
© 2003 Simon Robb

Typeset in Mrs Eaves 12/13pt by fat afternoon, Sydney
Printed in Australia by Carillon Graphic Communications, Sydney

National Library of Australia
Cataloguing-in-Publication data:

ISBN 0-646-42741-5

Title: Hulk, The

First edition 2003

Cover: photograph of the Hulk *Fitzjames* courtesy of the Mortlock Library

The writing and promotion of this book was assisted by the
South Australian Government through Arts South Australia.

This project has been assisted by the Federal Government through
the Australia Council, its arts funding and advisory body.

Now the Lord had prepared a Leviathan to swallow up Jonah.

By art is created that great Leviathan, called a Commonwealth or State — which is but an artificial man.

CONTENTS

INTRODUCTION

I have a confession for you, dear reader. I have found myself attracted to the story before you as a means of being moved to pity and awe, of experiencing, in my imagination at least, the thrall of darkness that alighted upon us when we were young, to experience once again the terror of power, the terror of separation, of cruelty that we could not conceive, and my confession is to say that I take pleasure in this terror. I enjoy the misery of others, I enjoy the crimes of the state, I enjoy the unjust punishment of the innocent. I am haunted by myself as a child and am reminded of a fear so great that I am moved to resolve and flee it all at once. I have flights of fancy where I feel myself soar and exalt and these flights take wing on the misery of others. I crush thousands in my wake. They exist in my mind, and on this page, and perhaps, even, within you too dear reader.

This story has its origins in a little known fact. In South Australia, from 1880 to 1891, boys sentenced to serve prison terms were incarcerated on the hulk *Fitzjames*, an old ship moored off the metropolitan coast of Adelaide. Up to sixty boys at a time would be kept on board. Their ages ranged from 8 to 16 years.

It is my argument, dear reader, that the hulk *Fitzjames* is both culturally familiar (it belongs to the convict history of Australia) yet appears where it is least expected, in a supposedly convict-free location (Adelaide). The appearance of something familiar in an unexpected place, in a place where it is meant to be impossible, evokes in all of us a sense of disorientation about our history and identity. This uncanny effect allows phantasies to inhabit the disrupted space of historical identity. With respect to the hulk *Fitzjames*, these are typically Gothic phantasies: feelings to do with entrapment, dread, violence, sexual excess and monsters. *The Hulk* that you have before you, dear reader, represents both these narrative phantasies and the historical conditions that allow them to flourish.

Boys were sent to the hulk primarily for criminal offences. Of the 39 newly committed boys in 1886, for example, 34 were sentenced for stealing (SAPP). The other main reason for committal was absconding from the Industrial School. Between 1880 and 1885 there were 22 boys transferred from the Industrial School to the hulk. Eighteen of these were originally sentenced to the Industrial School for being either uncontrollable or neglected. In all but one case the boys were transferred to the hulk for absconding from the Industrial School (Commission xxxix). The average age of these boys was 11 years.

In 1880 'neglected' referred to children who were begging, homeless, uncontrollable, living in brothels, with a thief, prostitute, or a drunkard. In colonial Adelaide neglected children could be detained in the Industrial School for between six months and seven years (Dickey 57-58). The most usual circumstance leading to admission (voluntary or under compulsion) was family poverty and the majority of admissions were from families where the father had deserted (Dickey 91).

The colonial state, dear reader, had powers to police the movements, habitation, and associations of boys and to place aberrant bodies in facilities where moral policing could be strictly enforced. The hulk *Fitzjames* was an integral part of this machinery of power and the historical documents of this machinery are an integral part of the textual field that I document here, for you, in *The Hulk*.

The historical textual field consists of a range of sources. The major published text is the *Second and Final Report of Commission Appointed to Report on the Destitute Act, 1881; Together with Minutes of Proceedings, Evidence, and Appendices (1885)*. This is the record of an extensive government inquiry into all facilities and personnel involved in the care, sentencing and reforming of children and adults in the State at that time. The report consists of transcripts of evidence taken during the inquiry, with additional statistical information. Documents from State archival sources and from contemporaneous newspaper reports are also used. Included in this is the *Register of Admissions to the Reformatory hulk Fitzjames*, the admissions journal used on the hulk. It lists the names of boys, their religion, parental history, date of committal, length of sentence and where a boy was sent at the end of his sentence. I reproduce in part these original works not only in the hope that they may reach a wider audience, but also that they may shed immediate light on the style of thinking and speaking that appertained to the conditions surrounding these poor boys.

Research of primary material pertinent to the hulk *Fitzjames* reveals the ways in which late colonial Australia produced reformed boys, yet there is no record whatsoever of the boys themselves. They exist only as the absent product of a set of rules governing mind, body, and soul. Their lived experience, their response to conditions, their internal life exists primarily in forms imagined or created from the recorded discourses of power. It was a ghost ship then that I had before me, of boys who uttered not a single word, whose words were dead, and I felt the need to reconstruct them. I am a person of some imagination, some would say a sickly excess, nevertheless I felt a strong desire to build a whole boy, without, I might add, a recourse to fabrication. I wanted, in part, to make these boys speak without fabrication or fiction. I wanted to hear something impossible, I wanted something impossible to appear, in the same way that the hulk *Fitzjames* appears in an uncanny way, where it is supposed to be impossible. I decided, therefore, to make these absent boys speak by using a method of substitution. The substitution involved a gathering of voices from boys, workers and managers who had experience with contemporary equivalents to the hulk. So I felt the need to move again in time, to post-colonial Adelaide, 1998, where there are two major facilities for the 'reforming' of boys who commit crime; 'Magill Training Centre' and 'Cavan Training Centre'. The South Australian Department of Family and Community Services is the government body administering these facilities and the body that approved a series of interviews with boys and staff at Cavan.

The interviews were calm and polite affairs, something akin to an ideal English tutorial at University. The simulated classroom within this situation was facilitated by my good-self utilising a non-judgmental interviewing style where questions oscillated between invitations towards narration, critical reflection and self-expression (Hunter). The boys were very willing and articulate students and similarly the interviews conducted with the manager of Cavan and one of the workers were straightforward and open. The material gathered was a document of the life lived in contemporary reformatories. It was, I believe, a true and faithful collection of readings of a lived text, carried out within an environment of attentive listening.

The other access that we have, dear reader, to boys sent to the hulk *Fitzjames*, is through the stories that they read. In particular I mean those stories found in the *Boys Own Annuals*, which were published in England, exported to Australia, and read by boys on the hulk (Commission). The Annuals assumed a male, juvenile audience, that had leisure time, wealth and education — none of which the hulk boys possessed in any great degree. In one sense, therefore, the Annuals could not speak in any direct manner to the boys on the hulk. Many of the stories, however, were adventures where the cental character (the boy) was challenged in terms of his moral beliefs, courage, and loyalty to family and friends. The challenges to identity acted out in these stories reverberated strongly with those being played out in the daily routines on the hulk. I would suggest, therefore, that particular stories enabled a boy to interpret his own position, in effect making the experience of the story one of pertinent self-reflection. This process must be balanced against an inevitable ironic distance that any reader must take up against a text when confronted by their own otherness. The stories, for the boys, would also be vehicles for an imaginative entry into identities and experiences whose remoteness and impossibility would only increase their exoticism and appeal. We may see these stories, therefore, as extant fragments of self reflection, ironic displacement and imaginative yearning. This, as of course you no doubt have gathered, is a contemporary reading which cannot be dis-entangled from the historical experiences of the stories. I have partially re-told these stories in *The Hulk* with an acknowledgment that they represent a historical experience informed by contemporary theory. The stories, their use by boys incarcerated on the hulk and their existence as objects of literary theory are all pertinent to the textual field of *The Hulk*.

What I have been calling, dear reader, the textual field, also exists as a real-life Gothic story about the identity of Adelaide. The existence of the hulk *Fitzjames* permits a florid eruption of Gothic phantasies, through which some readers may experience a sense of pleasurable liberation from their day to day identity. Gothic phantasies are saturated with heightened feeling or affect. Consider *Wuthering Heights, Frankenstein* and *Dracula*. This affective excess has its roots, without doubt, in Romanticism, and in the idealising notion that knowledge can be gained in a heightened, affective merging between self and other (McCarthy, cited in Kerr). The dominant tone, as we well know, of Romantic or Gothic writing, is of course sentimentality — an excess of refined, tender and mournful feelings circulating around struggles concerning knowledge of the other. In *The Hulk* a contemporary desire for knowledge concerning the hulk *Fitzjames* takes the form of a sentimental journey, akin to the Gothic narratives of the 19th century. A contemporary desire for knowledge, a desire that we must all, inevitably, partake of, through the form of the sentimental

Gothic, is a manifest feature of the textual field documented by *The Hulk* (see Kerr for further discussion on the relationship between commentary, knowledge and the sentimental).

There is a bleak presence latent in all sentimental merging, dear reader, a bleakness linked to knowledge since the time of Plato, and that bleakness has a name: paedophilia. When the desire for knowledge plays itself out in the form of a sentimental Gothic journey, and when that journey takes place within the context of a reformatory for boys, it is, regrettably, inevitable that paedophilia will be present. This aspect of the textual field does not come directly from any historical source, nor does it come lightly from my pen, but is the inevitable result of the contemporary imagination confronted by certain uncanny historical conditions. Paedophilia is an extreme case of a sentimental desire for knowledge, and is likewise a gross abuse of power that produces affects resonant with those associated with the Gothic genre: feelings to do with entrapment, dread, violence, sexual excess and monsters.

I have, reader, often referred to the term textual field, but that term could just as soon be substituted by another — mystory (Ulmer). In each of these cases the object of study is the principle source for the structure and content of the author's commentary. The secondary text, or commentary, takes its cue from the specific configuration of its object, rather than accede to a generalised theory of knowledge. The task, dear reader, of 'mystory' is to recognise the kinds of stories that go to make up the experience of the object of study —its textual field—and to develop a relationship between them in a site-specific form. Perhaps a better way to put this is that the task of the expert, their central organising function, is demonstrably de-centred, placed in the background, organising the 'paradigm of possibilities', as Ulmer puts it. This type of ethically ambitious, even utopian literary experiment has, to my knowledge, likewise been described as fictocriticism (see Nettelbeck; King).

So now I have been straight with you. I can tell you that this is no clean-cut narrative. These boys have life in greater and lesser motives. I have confused, somewhat, the origin and cause of *The Hulk*. I have at times been unable to progress without some fabrication. Indeed I am all fabrication at times, and would not want it any other way. I can say, in my defence, that these base progressions are examples of the original story moving through the humours of a modern man like yourself, and that I am admitting to nothing other than the generative means of any so-called history.

THE AUTHOR'S ENCOUNTER
WITH A FORMER SUPERINTENDENT
OF THE HULK *FITZJAMES*

My story begins the day of my encounter with a former superintendent of the hulk *Fitzjames*. He was working at the rear of his carpentry shop. I saw him just as he was putting down his plane. He wiped his hands upon his apron and stood still. Then he looked my way.

'What would you want from me?' he said.

'I am writing of those who were aboard the hulk *Fitzjames*. I had some information that I may find such a person here.'

I may just as well had been a thief of souls as an author to this man. His apprehension was palpable, as if he had been through many interviews before and had not liked them much at all.

'What kind of writer might you be?' he asked.

'I am an honest one, I believe.'

'Yes, but how is it that you write?'

'I am guided by some principles. At other times I give free rein to my hand. I fashion information into a narrative, and that narrative is structured around a desire to come close to my reader, feelingly. Above all my want is to instil within them some feeling that life can be worthwhile.'

'So you write romantically?'

'I trust not.'

'I think that you do. Now answer me this, what is it about the hulk that draws you ?'

'It is its blackness. It is as if for years some dark thing from fiction was afloat in the material world. It is the fact of boys being imprisoned on a thing of dark fantasy. The feelings that it touches lie too deep. They are too hard to bring to the surface. I feel these things and I feel very close to being there, in some strange way.'

'You want to use me to get these feelings out? Do you believe I want to be used in this way? Do you even know who I am?'

'I would like to know.'

'I am John Redman, one time superintendent on the hulk.'

Feelings of great joy and foreboding swept through me. To appear calm and rational, I concentrated my energies on the materiality of the scene. On the fact of two bodies speaking in the present.

The thrall of the past and its imaginary power, putting this to one side, I asked him if he would talk with me.

'With all due respect, you strike me as being too naive. Heightened sensibilities are useless for these times. What we need today is analytical narrative. I do not see it in you.'

There was a silence then that could have meant the end of my inquiries. Mr. Redman was in two minds, I could sense that. After some time he walked towards the ladder at the rear of the workshop. 'Come with me upstairs. I have finished here for now. You can ask me what you want about the hulk. Whether I will answer is another thing.'

Some time later Mr. Redman spoke at last, breaking the dreary silence. 'I have led you to believe that I will talk with you about my time upon the hulk. But I have had enough with boys. Therefore, I am sorry to say that I shall not take up the opportunity to have an interview with you.'

His statement left me feeling rather flat. He had been rather badly treated by the Way Commission, I do believe, and still felt the soreness of the wound. I had heard that there was something of a conspiracy of one class against another in it. I suggested as much to him, but there was only an uncomfortable movement of his hands from place to place, and the awkward beginnings of some indecipherable reply.

And then Mr. Redman fell silent. And it was a silence that began to fill the room, as if it leaked out from him. It was a coldness that I felt. He stared at a picture hanging from the wall opposite, which depicted, I noticed for the first time, a carpenter's workshop. In the workshop was a sturdy man and a young boy. The man was demonstrating something to the boy. A way of shaving or refining a piece of rough wood. The boy was all attention and willingness to learn. His eyes were open and wide to any lesson that he may pick up. I took the picture to be an exemplar of tutelage, of the delights of apprenticeship between a master craftsman and a youth. Mr. Redman seemed to be quite lost to the rest of the room. The word 'sentimental' came to mind. It was a great discomfort to me to witness Mr. Redman in this state. I was about to excuse myself from his company when he spoke.

And it was a voice that agonised about its return to this world. It was the voice of a near-drowned man roused back to life.

'I will show you where one former boy lives,' he said. But before we left he informed me that he had something to give me...

I waited in the strange room, wondering if he would return at all. When he did re-appear, it was with a large bound book.

'Take this. I no longer want it. Use it as you will. Be sure to be fair with your treatment of it. I do not want to be made to look a fool again.' With that he handed me the book. As I leafed through its pages, I became aware that this book was in fact a journal, kept whilst on board the hulk. This was a sensational discovery for me, but before I could say a word he had already begun his descent, down the steep ladder, and out towards the former boy...

We're walking some way down the streets of Alberton when Mr. Redman takes my arm and points across the road.

'That's where he lives.'

'Who' I say.

'James Burns' says he.

Mr. Redman stands next to me, quite close, and I feel the warmth of his body, almost pressing, but not quite, against me. I feel his urging to go forward.

'Are you not curious,' he says, 'don't you wish to go inside?'

I am hesitant. It is a pleasant enough place and I am wanting so dearly to go inside. I nod my head slowly and dreamily in reply. My legs I find are carrying me across the road and through the gate. I pass red geraniums and purple agapanthus. I knock and, as I do, find the door to be ajar. There is something strange here. I go inside. It is almost empty. There are strong stale smells. There's an aqua-marine wall, and a hole in the floor-boards stuffed with newspaper, that has become yellow. And wet. That's the smell. Wet yellow paper. I walk down the hallway. I look up and see, slowly floating down, pieces of cream paint. Also, there are enormous cracks in the cornices. Giant cobwebs hang from the ceiling. Now I'm in his bedroom. I'm sure of that. It is an almost empty room with a bed against the corner of the far wall. I feel a certain immoral feeling here. As if the bed were dangerous. The covers are unmade. They do not want to be made. Old and woollen, I think, some kind of purple with woven knots. There is as well a large bound volume lying on the bed. It is at that instance that I am chilled by another being present. I am struck by it. I turn slowly to see. It wavers before me, revealing a more defined, essential shape, of some soldier, leaning on the barrel of a gun. He is strong and handsome. He has a good smile. I am certain it is James Burns. I walk around stupidly. Keeping my distance from him. I want to open the window. I am transfixed, yet I cannot resist the large bound book that lies upon his bed. I tremble towards it. I take the volume in my hands and see that it is a scrap-book. Inside it is the name 'Alfred Weippert'. The book has pictures torn from magazines, also, there is much handwriting here. I'm reading the writing, next to the pictures. I'm reading and I hear the door close at front. This is terror to my soul. I grip the book and am frozen. I turn to see standing in the hallway, a dark figure...

And then the fit came upon me. It is often at times of great stress that I suffer the fit. It is a seizure of the brain and it takes me over entirely. I become quite dead to the world. I can recall these physic journeys sometimes, and sometimes I am all blank. A black thing without recall. Only this time it was that I found myself on fire. I was burning and suspended above some water. I let go my hold on the sky and dropped fast into the wet dark cold. And then I struggled once more into the night. In the distance I saw the hulk. Black. Immense. Moving up and down from the water's force. I wanted so much to be there. But I felt myself being drawn, against my desires, away from the dark ship. This was a true agony. Perhaps I was not yet prepared enough. Or it was from some other cause that I did not know. Either way I was carried towards land, northwards, to the end of Lefevre's Peninsula. Flat land bordered by mangroves. That also contained secrets. And corpses. Bloated from first settlement. Just north-east of the hulk. I'm seeing boy spirits, who have come here at night. I can see them vanishing into the stars. Purposeful. Honest. Guiltless. Fraternal. I am moved by the graciousness of their bodies. Who have departed this incarcerating world. Who move through clouds of solar wind. Incredible velocities flee the peninsula. A boy tells me that he needs to come here. That he regrets having to return to where he is hopeless. To the dark ship and to the hopeless body. Adrift. Aimless. Secret. Fugitive. He's vanished from my side. He's emersed himself in the sky. I see him somersaulting above clouds of dust. I seem to have arrived at the end of the known earth.

Abruptly from that place I am taken, in my dream body, back to Alberton, escorted there by some unknown boy, to my prone shell, lying empty on the floor of a stranger's house. As he departs I faintly hear him say: 'take the scrap-book with you.'

 It was the hand of Mr. Redman that next I felt upon me. Gentle slaps and conciliatory tones greeted me as I returned to the conscious world. I looked around the room. It had lost its hallucinatory glow. Then it began to dawn on me, that in my heightened state, I had misread things once again.

     'I believe I became disorganised and fretful about James Burns.'

     'There was no James Burns present,' said Mr. Redman.

     I looked again at the portrait.

     'I am so foolish. I had taken this dreary portrait to be a spiritual apparition.'

     'It is time for you and I to go,' said he.

As we did so I recalled the admonition of the boy. I know dear reader that I am revealing some unpleasant personal details here. That I am not only weak and suggestible to fevers of the brain, but worse, am led on by this sickness to acts of petty larceny. Be that as it may, I took possession of the scrap-book.

'I see that you are a thief as well,' said Mr. Redman, 'make sure you return that text when you are done, it may be more precious than you know.'

We stepped away from the portrait's gaze and moved swiftly to the daylight outside…

THE JOURNAL OF JOHN REDMAN, SUPERINTENDENT OF THE HULK *FITZJAMES*, 1883 TO 1884

14th March, 1883

Arrived to find school being led by a fourteen year old by the name of George Higgins. He had been having a high time. On my insistence he demonstrated a typical lesson. Made good a blow-hard master, standing before the blackboard, with reader in hand, spouting Latin and commanding obedience. Asked this grand boy what he had been sent to the hulk for. He was quite straight with his reply: 'forgery and uttering, Sir.' Higgins had been given the job by Mr. Alton, the previous superintendent. Curious indeed. I am determined to amend this situation and to teach the boys all I can. Am most anxious about this, but it must be done.

15th March, 1883

Mr. Alton seems to have established a regular pattern for the boys. Must get this clear for myself. Mr. Button is obliging me in this dictation. Boys rise at 6.30. One squad is told off to make the beds or bring the bedding up for airing. Another party is told off to clean the knives, forks and boots. Yet another group to wash the main deck. Boys are thus occupied until breakfast time. Then prayers are read. They kneel down and repeat the Lord's prayer. After breakfast half hour's drill. Then the boys go into the workshop. School boys start lessons at 10 and they go until 11.30. Again between 1.30 and 3.30. In between times there would be jobs around the ship to be done. I give the lessons. Think I can remember that. In my cabin at the long table. Cosy. Note: five or six boys from the workshop to go ashore for provisions. From 12 to one there is dinner and play time. Then workshop or school. Supper at 5.30. After supper they play until dark. They draw, paint, play draughts. Sometimes they have the magic lantern. Then they go down below and read. At 8 they have prayers and bed.

(Mr. Redman mentions magic lantern slides. What were they watching? Boys seem to be objects of a schedule. I assume that they were experiencing this. That they experienced life as an object of the authority exercised against them. Without their consent, of course. Things that are moved around and detained as sub-sections of the order of things. Must look for indications, other than the incident of George Higgins, that they acted in some contrary way.)

16th March, 1883

Mr Button takes me to the boot and shoe workshop. Twenty six lads, varying in age from 9 to 15, were busily employed cutting, pegging, soling and heeling boots and shoes of various sizes. They manage to turn out from twenty eight to thirty pairs per week. Enough for the wants of the sixty seven boys who live on the *Fitzjames*, and for the old people at the Destitute Asylum. The work is not up to the highest standard, but it is plain and substantial withal. In the tailoring establishment some thirty-two youngsters were making shirts, vests, and other garments. It appears they make enough for the requirements of the hulk and also of the Industrial School at Magill. A first-class London cutter might smile at the button holes of the waistcoat. He might laugh at the general build of the trousers. They will, Mr. Button assures me, pass muster with novices, and will probably last quite as long as the best tailor made.

16th March, 1998

Mr Button and I then proceeded to a tiny cell, in the hold of hulk. 'This is the camera room', he said. 'We can take a picture if we're worried about a boy, and we do that when we're worried about a boy, we don't do it all the time, so the boy's know about the cameras in the camera room, they know why they're in there, they know why the cameras are there. It's usually if they're trying to hurt themselves, those sort of reasons.'

The camera room is a tiny cell with a fold away plank for a bed there is a small window letting in light and sea air. At one end of the room high up is what I assumed to be the opening for the taking of photographs. On the floor found traces of hair, milk and blood.

Mr. Button guides me down to the control room. 'All the systems come home here to roost' he said, pointing to a bench top containing lights, switches and bells. 'Thompson over there can monitor the perimeter. You noticed there weren't any walls or bars or fences. We monitor things. At night there's a beam set up around the place. Not so that we know what boys escape, but mainly to know if anybody's trying to come in.'

Mr. Button seems more concerned about boys entering than escaping, making the hulk out to be more desirable than repugnant.

Whilst in the control room I began to look through this and that piece of dusty trash and old pieces of information until I came upon a series of photographs. At first I could see almost nothing in them and thought them worthless, poorly lit and amateurish. On closer inspection however could see faces, clouds and flowers.

Exhausted and frail I proceeded with my guide further down the hulk to the 'cabin' or 'dark cell'. 'This is called a cabin', said he, 'we call them cabins. It's monitored. If a boy is out of control, if he's not able to control his behaviour, if he's fighting then they come in here until they can cool down and control themselves. When they've got the ability to say yeah I can go into my bedroom, it's Ok I'm alright now, then they go.

The use of this cabin is very infrequent. I don't think once a
week we use it. But we keep a record of all the use, how long
a boy's in here. The youth workers can only keep them in here
for one hour, they need to get permission for any longer than
that from you, sir, any longer than eight hours you have to go
to your director, but usually boys are in here ten minutes,
just till they can get hold of themselves. So when they're ready
to come out they tell. All this is recorded and all the use of
this is recorded, so the bell rings not only in the unit, but at
the front control desk, so it rings in two places, if it's not
answered in the unit then the control room answers it. It's
important because if anything happens to a boy you need to
know, what happened, what led up to it, you know if there's
a Coronial inquiry…'

I saw in the dark cell the traces of marks and scratches on the
surface of the wall. On closer inspection the marks appeared
to take on the form of a scene. In that barely perceptible scene
were two children standing in a forest, holding hands. They
simply stood, fearfully, in the shadow of an ominous pine.
In the distance was a hut with a chimney. A sallow light spilled
from out its stack. As the other members of the party left the
room I stood quite still and saw a shadowy figure inside the
tree looking directly into my eyes.

2nd April, 1883

The night watch is kept by two old men from the Destitute
Asylum, whose duty is to be on deck in turn to attend to the
ship's light. Have concerns employing paupers in any capacity
in an institution for training children. Lads are likely to be
contaminated by pauperising influences. Am informed that
one of the old men from the Asylum who left the hulk had
been notorious at Port Adelaide for his immorality. In one
case, at least, there has been the same want of care in the
selection of a petty officer. The man had been prosecuted for
rape and was living an openly immoral life.

19th July, 1883

Wilhelm Cumme apprenticed from hulk, going to farmer for 3 years. Had served 17 months on board. Will be 16 at expiry of indentures. Good boy.

(He only supplies the building blocks for a bland boy. Trust there is some other boy aboard.)

21st July, 1883

Welcome Mr Weippert aboard the hulk as the new teacher. He has many charms and seems to be well liked by the lads.

2nd August, 1883

Edwin Humby and James Mannoo. Both apprenticed from hulk, going to salt manufacturer, Yorke Peninsula. Humby had served 13 months on board. Indentured for 3 years. Fair boy. Mannoo had served 19 months. Will be 17 when finished apprenticeship. Mannoo originally sentenced to Industrial School for stealing four pounds of resin. Strange crime. Bad boy.

6th August, 1883

Fair day. Slight wind. Birds some nuisance again. Received James Burns. Age 8. Youngest boy on board, ever, I believe. Had absconded four times in just one week from Industrial School. Found wandering about in city. Looking for his home. Father is deceased. Given up to Industrial School as an uncontrollable boy by his mother just 10 days previous. Is an extremely sad boy. Has no other family here. I believe he feels very afraid. I feel the need to keep an eye out for him. Does not look well or at all hopeful. Keeps saying that he is ready to go home to his mother. I tell him that he cannot. That he is in my care now. Cried at this news. Other boys fell silent as they saw this. Remembered themselves, I believe. Ship's company fell silent, feeling as one. Remembering being abandoned and so on. I tell them that I will help them all to be good chaps

and to have some sort of future. Some are heartened by this.
I return to the cabin. Melancholy. Do not know if this is a
such a good enterprise to be with.

(He seems here to be using the boy to appear to be a worthwhile fellow. Boys used
to construe author as being one of great empathy. Adding to the mystique of
leadership. Using boy's feelings to effect sympathy in the reader. Is this for
understanding the position of the boy, or for justifying the authority of the man?)

11th November, 1883

Receive threatening letters from Mr. Humby. States he will
burn down the hulk. Incensed about his son's apprenticeship
to salt mine. Forward following letter as some comfort.

Dear Sir

*As to your inquiries regards the boy Edwin Humby. I told him I wanted him to
write me a short letter, and he sullenly replied that 'He did not know what to
write about'. We discussed various topics, some of which were acceptable. I then
asked him if he was happy and comfortable, and he said, 'Yes.' 'Write that then,'
I said. 'Are you doing your best to learn and to make yourself useful?' He said
'yes', and again I said, 'write that'. Subsequently I saw the lad's box and found
pipes and tobacco in it. When I saw him I remonstrated with him for smoking,
and he said 'he could not work without it.' I then asked him if he was well
treated, and again he said, 'yes.' I asked him if I was to tell his father he was
well and happy, and he said he was, but would like to go home. I asked would he
like to go back to the hulk and he said, 'No.' Mr. Telfer came out then, and I
told him about the smoking. 'Oh, let him 'ave his smoke. He thinks it does him
good.' I should have stopped it, but I did not want to be unkind. The boy's letter
is as follows:*

Port Vincent Saltworks
October 11th, 1883

Dear Sir - Since I been here I been engaged engine driving,
wood cutting, salt shredding, and other preparations for the
aquaculture of salt. I am quite happy and comfortable here,
and am doing my best to be useful.

I remain yours etc.

Looking at the orthography and phraseology of the letter, you might think it has the marks of a letter that has been dictated, certainly, indicating perhaps that the letter was not composed or written by the boy. But at the time of composing the boy said, 'What shall I write?' I said, are you happy here?' and he said, 'Yes, I am.' 'Then,' I said, 'write that.'

I hope that this letter will enlighten you as to his character and disposition.

I am yours sir, etc.
Inspector for the Lower Yorke Peninsula

12th December, 1883

Two more boys arrive. Sent down for rape and indecent assault. Do not think these boys should be here. Or at least that some other way of keeping them on board be hit upon. They are not a good influence. James Morris is only twelve yet he seems to glory in his crime. He is a very bold boy and seems to encourage in others the desire to do the same. Have asked the night wardens to keep a special eye out for him. Immoral acts in the dormitories cannot be tolerated. Yet it seems impossible to stamp this out. The dormitories, as at present arranged, are more likely to encourage improper conduct than to check it. Boys and double bunks, I feel, are an unsavoury admixture. Also, must be rid of partition that stops warden from seeing whole of the boys at once. It is so unnatural, all of this, I despair for a solution.

(If Mr. Redman was a worldly man he would not use the boys in this manner. He is simply afraid of that which we all know goes on between young boys in close together. He is simply using them to appear more moral and lawful than all else. Though he would need to construct things in this way. It was, and still is, not possible to be too public about either the extent or even the existence of these things. I think that the recent trial of Mr. Wilde sent all of us a salutatory lesson concerning the relationship between writing and the law. Despite that, these boys come out from Redman's hand as licentious and wanton. But think of another way around it. Boys would be experiencing themselves as objects of moral surveillance. They would feel then that some immoral interplay was a way of being free.)

15th February, 1884

Have returned from one week in prison. Boys seem to treat me differently. Have heard laughter behind my back. Gaol was a nightmare. Unruly and rough.

Worse than all my years at sea. Feeling ashamed. I hope these feelings pass.

(Author makes a remarkable admission. I do not know why he was in jail, only that the reason seems to not have been too serious. He seems to be immune from all irony. The criminal in charge of the criminal. Expect no stones to be thrown from this point on. Silences in his writing I am doubly wary of now. Would want to hide his own untenable position. Secondly, could not admit that the boys knew him as a hypocrite of the first degree. Boys' spirits would soar from this knowledge, I am sure. All aboard participants in epic jape. Boys given great lesson in the ways of authority. A power of good towards their reform.)

2nd March 1884

Visit from Archdeacon Farr. Arrives at dinner time, as is his habit. Tells me he would like to chat with boys. Boys warm to his presence. They want to be seen by him. Chatted with boys. Asked if they thought they needed more sunshine. The hulk is in a perpetual gloom due to the fact that an awning covers over the entire deck area. Boys replied that yes, they would. Leads boys in prayers before meal. He waits with the boys for his share of the meat and pudding. Sits quietly with them as they eat. The sun sets. Calm emanates all around.

4th March, 1998

What I would like for boys when they leave here is to understand that they do have options, and that they can think for themselves. To understand that the ways that they've been thinking and acting in the past have meant that they've ended up in lock-up. And if they don't want to come back to lock-up then they're going to have to make some decisions about thinking and acting differently when they get back out there. Rehabilitation means that you are fixing something that's broken. And I don't think these boys are broken. And I don't think they need fixing. But there is another word, 'remediation'. That implies assisting in areas where there is a lack or a need. So really that's the mission here. If boys can't read or write, we try and teach them to read and write. If they can't manage their anger we work with them on that if they want to work on it. If they have a problem with drug and alcohol use in the community we work with them on that. There's a staff member here who uses a boating analogy. We'll row the boat to you but you really need to row it back. There's a lot of different boats we have to row here, to try to encourage them in that game of developing themselves. Yes so it is about helping them reach standards that they want to reach for themselves. And most of the boys do want to reach standards.

28th March, 1884

Receive notice that David Dee is being treated at the lunatic asylum. David Dee exhibited strange and eccentric behaviour which was certainly associated with constant and repeated self-abuse. Prior to admission to the hulk both David Dee and John Wallace committed unnatural offences together in the park lands.

There is nothing that has such debilitating effect on the constitution of the lower classes as immoral conduct.

It is the cause of insanity, epilepsy, and other derangements of the system.

2nd April, 1884

The Way Commission has been taking evidence from Mr. Reed concerning conditions on board the hulk. I am to be called some time in August. I am worried about my appearance there. The commissioners I have heard are out to get a new man for superintendent. I am not prepared to let this job go lightly from me. I have good work to do here, although it is trying, and I have of late felt somewhat over-burdened by my duties.

Receive letter from Archdeacon Farr re. improvements to hulk.

Dear sir,

As you know I have been in the habit of visiting the hulk on and off for two and half years now. I have also seen many other reformatory institutions, both here in the colonies and in the mother country, and France. All in all our hulk is not up to the same standard as say The Formidable, the Vernon or Mettray. In every one of those institutions there is a pride among the inmates in the place they are in. They do not simply look upon themselves as criminal boys who are to be kept under restraint, but they have a feeling that they are to be helped to raise themselves, and that they can do it. They are encouraged to feel a sense of honour about the place and themselves. They are rewarded publicly for their good efforts. But at the hulk the boys are hidden away and are not classified nor encouraged to feel a sense of pride in any achievements they make. From the Formidable and the Vernon boys will nearly always be employed at sea, and from Mettray the boys will be taken into the French army. They are employed by the state after having been helped by it. But our hulk does none of this and farms the boys to private interests who can then exploit them for personal gain. The boys have a sense then that their self development is for other's private gain rather than to benefit the community and the wider society. I cannot help thinking you would do a great deal with the boys, which would help raise them, if you required them to dress in a really nice uniform after a certain time of the day, and that when their work was over they should be taught to look upon themselves as having some little pride in themselves and their appearance. I think also that a band would be a good thing there. I do not think that the privy accommodation is quite as good as it should be, but there may have been alterations since I was last there.

yours &c
Geo. Farr.

My dear George,

I would like to re-assure you that all Christian measures are being taken for the guidance and well-being and pride of the boys. The privy has been changed since you were last there and your suggestion of a band is a good one. I think a drum and fife band might be a fine idea. Also, you will be interested to note, as a means of illustrating the point, that I received not long ago a letter concerning a hulk boy, written by the father. The boy was engaged as steward on board a vessel, and had reached London. His uncle, a leading Baptist minister, wrote to the father expressing his surprise at the manifest sincerity and Christian piety and his refinement of manners, considering the comparatively meagre education he necessarily received. And his other relatives all wrote in the same manner. He gratefully attributed the desirable change in the young man's tastes and manners to the mingled kindness and firmness which I showed to him. Additionally my tact and discernment of character proved to him that I am in the right place in the government service, and that, for the good of the colony, I may long find such service congenial to my tastes. That boy was a good one for me he was always doing what was wanted. I took him over to my small cupboard I had and I gave him my sweets and a bit of fruit. I said to him that he would get a reward for being good to me and he did. He would put on the model dress I had made for him. And he would bring me my brandy. And cake. And he would say, here sir is your refreshment. He was very Christian in his kindness because he would clean my shoes for me when I said they looked dirty.

He would bring me my tea and I would say I think my shoes are dirty boy, you may like to clean them and rub them. And he would. And I would give him some more fruit because he liked it. I would recommend that boy's kindness and firmness to anyone who asked me. I myself have always tried to give the boys the proper tastes of life. He should be a good steward that boy because he has the history here of manners. Most importantly he took pride in his dress, which as you suggest, is a sure route to success in the after life.

I am yours
in Christian piety
the Superintendent.

1st May, 1884

Peaceful autumn day. No wind. Boys seem well today.
Received two more transfers from Industrial School. Herbert
Dolan (age 13) and John Connell (age 11). Warrants of
transfer make interesting reading. Boys had acted together
to steal threepence. Absconded from Industrial School and
later found to be living with aboriginals. Sentenced to hulk
for that crime. Why do they do this? Have been having
trouble with dark presence reported by boys. Do not know
what to make of it. I am suspicious but have had Mr. Button
confirm that he has heard uncanny noises in hold at night.
Will investigate further.

(Is he referring to dark presence that is a fact or a fabrication of the boys? That the
boys may be fabricators of ghost stories is hardly surprising. That they would use
these stories to move their masters hither and thither is a little more to the point.
Even more interesting is the confirmation by Mr. Redman. Perhaps the boys were
so determined about the supernatural that they willed its presence on board the
hulk. Or that they wanted fear to be there, manifestly so, for the others to witness,
as if they were composing a memorandum: 'here is a manifestation of the fearful
presence on board. It is fact. What are you to do with it?')

10th May 1884

Mr Weippert's conduct has become somewhat erratic. See him
occasionally as a shadowy figure, at night, moving across the
deck. The other night I hailed him and insisted that he answer
me. He told me that he suffered from insomnia and could
sometimes do nothing at night other than wander in an attempt
to hasten sleep with fatigue. I cautioned him about the
appearance of his conduct. Told him to seek out Pastor Bamber.

13th May, 1884

The Way Commission continues preliminary investigations.
I have decided to make a few changes to the diet. Give milk in
the tea and cocoa twice a week, instead of tea at every meal.
Also (another change) they get treacle every evening and
dripping for breakfast.

(Boys are taught another lesson. Food is not simply nutrition, but is part of the compact between the ruler and the ruled. Their health is subject to the feelings that those who rule them have about their power, and so forth, so that generally, they have no certainty at all that they should live.)

2nd June, Sunday, 1884

Surprise visit from Messrs. Adamson and Davis. Most unfortunate. Was in my cabin with sever cold at time of their arrival. Mr. Button walking the poop and the gangway sentry was absent. Most embarrassing that they arrived without any official welcome. Simply got on board amid great hubbub from boys. Visitors saw straight off four boys standing with faces to the cabin for misconduct. They were rightfully punished. I see no harm in this sort of discipline. Why do I worry? Must remember to punish the sentry. Visitors were eager to learn how boys spent their Sundays. Talked to one boy who was reading an old magazine and another who had an old book. Mr. Davis stated to my face that these boys were miserable. I stood my ground and flatly said that they were not. We attended the service for the Protestant children held by Pastor Bamber. Much yawning and restlessness. Two boys stood up for misconduct during prayers. Lesson to do with 'whoso breaketh an hedge a serpent will bite him.' Boys seemed to take this in. Am I the serpent? Mr. Adamson commented that it was a sensible discourse, but mainly fired over the heads of the boys. Last hymn sung with gusto. Much rejoicing at end. Overheard one visitor say to the other that the singing was most wretched and miserable. Felt wounded by this. Wanted so much for the boys to be appreciated for their efforts. Feeble though they may be. They do not have a cultivated voice, which is the privilege of the few, who would be better using it to benefit, rather than condemn, others less fortunate. At the end of service toured visitors around the vessel. I have great worries about the outcome of this visit. Fear that they are agents for the Way Commission and want to do me in.

(Has the author any understanding at all? Why would the boys want to indicate that all was well, when, in front of witnesses, they had the chance to make a fool of their superiors? That they are not fully obedient to the arts of singing, is this not a way for them to still be somewhat free?)

16th June 1884

Very difficult evening. Called down to the lower quarters by the night wardsman. There I found Mr Weippert and Mr Jefferson in obvious moral disarray. Ordered them both to my cabin. Interrogation revealed nature of their night visitations. I have suspected Mr Weippert for some months now of being an unnatural man. I thought that his strange and uncanny behaviour could be tolerated to some degree given the nature of his medical condition and the unusual circumstances of the hulk itself. I find in the man the inability to overcome the moral fracture that I suffer from. I do not let him know this. I find something strangely compelling in him. I allow the man one more chance at transcending that which impels him towards his destruction.

21st June, 1884

Have received copy of letter sent by Messrs. Adamson and Davis to Destitute board re. visit to hulk. They had said that there was a great need for new books on board. I quote: 'we inspected those on board and think that if it was desired to give the boys a thorough distaste to reading, it would be difficult to make a better selection.' Have since then had donation of some new books. Thought though that the *British Workman* and *Band of Hope* were quite adequate for Sunday reading. Boys seem pleased at addition of *Boys Own Annual*. Have received back-issues dating from 1880.

(Mr. Redman seems not to understand that there are those of us who would rather be dead than be reading *Band of Hope*. This is not a man who does much good reading. His cultured guests had seen that at once. Boys would be experiencing themselves, up until the addition of the new books, as characters in the most limited and banal of narratives.)

23rd June 1884

Mr Weippert again of concern, most strange. Last night, late, I was awoken by a strange and unearthly sound coming from outside my cabin window. It was a shuffling noise not dissimilar

to that made by a shackled man moving. I opened my cabin
window to the sea and was astounded to see Mr Weippert
fleeing at inhuman speed along the outside of the hulk,
gripping the ship's planks, as if he were some creature.
I was too astounded to utter a single sound. Whence I had
composed myself the figure had vanished from sight.

24th June, 1884

Strange indecent. Two Commissioners return to the hulk.
Mr Goode said that they would like to see the official
documents of the hulk, in particular the records of admissions.
We subsequently passed down a long corridor filled with
shelves. Stacked high were pamphlets, books and documents
of various kinds. I wound back the compactor to reveal
another long passage-way lined with texts. Someway down the
passage-way our journey stopped. 'Ordinarily the volume lives
just up there', I said, 'on the top shelf. It share its quarters
with a lot of Lands Department indexes, and funnily enough,
a box of lunatic asylum records.' As I spoke Mr Goode reached
between the said texts and removed a large brown book.
'We've got here the *Register of Admissions to the Reformatory hulk
Fitzjames*', he said. 'It's a volume about two inches thick, by
about one foot long. It's a hand-written volume. First entry
in the book, as you would know Mr. Superintendent, is for
Alfred Stokes, age ten. He's described as a native aboriginal.
Late place of residence is given as the far north. His parents
are given as dead and religion none. He was sentenced to the
Reformatory hulk until he achieved the age of 16 for being
found unlawfully wandering about, having no home or settled
place of abode. Thereupon he was apprenticed to Mr. Robert
Best of Normanville. 'I notice, superintendent', said Mr Haines,
'that on release Alfred Stokes' nationality is given as English
and his religion is given as Protestant. Was the boy so reformed
by you that he was turned from a native person of no religion
to an Englishman of Protestant faith?' I muttered something
about the sentences being made by someone else and took

leave to use the water closet. The more I stayed put, the longer I became immobilised by confusion and shame.

26th June, 1884

Have placed Mr Weippert under close arrest on board and await the arrival of the police to escort him away. His conduct has become too obvious to ignore and will bring scandal to this institution if I do not act and condemn him now. His journal I have also taken in hand. Repulsive. Hideous man. Know now that this man was...what he was...I cannot name it. Odious fabricator. Deceitful. Used words. Cannot name the thing.

28th June, 1884

Am beginning to fear that some terrible retribution is coming. Have gone back to my Bible but find more disturbance than comfort in it. Read Isaiah 27.1: 'In that day the Lord with his great and strong sword shall punish Leviathan, the piercing serpent; he shall slay the dragon that is in the sea.'

30th June, 1884

In preparation for the Way Commission. Have been going over, in thorough manner, reasons for committal to hulk. List them here for future reference. For every one hundred boys that we have had here the following figures are correct. Neglected and uncontrollable...Twenty eight. Absconding from situation... Two. Offences against property...Sixty six. Offences against the person... Four. I cannot say that being uncontrollable or neglected is much of an offence. If the laws were more forgiving of boys who suffer for no fault of their own we would see far less of them incarcerated aboard. It would cut a good third of the boys away from the vessel.

(Does he reveal that he has insight into injustice, or, that he uses those unjustly treated to prove the necessity of the incarceration of the guilty. Is that plain? It were as if the incarceration of this boy was the fault of that boy. Must have been that way. That some boys were looked upon as being both a cause, and result, of criminal behaviour. That they carried a greater burden than their crime alone. I think those boys would have experienced themselves as carriers of some disease.)

20th July, 1884

It is my personal belief that I am indeed a right and proper person for the reformation of the boys and that my endeavours are unfairly maligned. I believe that there is nothing short of a class conspiracy motivating attacks upon my good self. It appears to me that the establishment in Adelaide cannot abide the idea that a self-taught man like myself could be capable of successfully reforming the young. To admit to that is to suggest that the educated upper classes do not have a monopoly on moral rightness. To admit that is to undermine, in part, the claim to 'natural' authority that these classes make for themselves. They cannot stand to see a fellow who is not of their own kind occupying their 'God-given' position of authority.

14th August, 1884

Suffered first day at Way Commission yesterday. I am their target, I know this. Made me say that, no, I had no training as a teacher, I was only ever a ship's carpenter, and yes, the divisions of the boys into classes made no material difference but still I would persist with it. I am their fool. Bad noises again coming from hold. Went down to investigate, at night, with the watchman. Could find nothing except usual creaks and leaks that one would expect. Still I am uneasy. Watchman said he would prefer to not be there. Says that he too feels uneasy.

21st August, 1884

Yesterday spent at the Way Commission. Am still exhausted from this. Spent troubled night and hardly slept. They seem to want to destroy me. Questions seemed to be of a persecutory nature. Almost insane. Kept asking me about towels and combs and tubs for the boys. Asked me how many combs were on board ship, as if I were superintendent of combs, above all else. Also, asked me if the combs were used promiscuously by the boys. Felt obliged to reply that yes, they were. I do not how they had gained intelligence of this. They bring up my week in gaol. As if this made me unfit to hold my position.

25th August, 1884

Return of the Way Commissioners to the hulk. Take them both to my cabin. Excuse myself to use the water closet. After some considerable time Mr Goode inquired as to my well being. 'Quite well now', I said. He asked me to rejoin them and as I stepped outside he brandished this book in my face and told me straight out that its pages would condemn me. I looked at him quite coolly saying that they were rightfully my property and that he should hand them over at once. The second commissioner intervened, setting Mr Goode straight about the ownership of the sentences. Thereupon I said that some writing was authentic while some was as a form of written relaxation or fantasy. He asserted that only a low man would could use words in this way and that I had penned my last sentence. At that moment the second commissioner intervened stating that the matter would be reviewed in proper time in the course of the proceedings of the commission and that the correspondence may be used as evidence by the commissioners. At that point I slumped in my chair, looking for all the world like a dead man.

27th August, 1884

Another dreary day. Overcast. Slept late again. Having great difficulty in getting out from my cabin. I do not have the energy to be with the boys.

Feel that I may collapse.

That would be bad.

To just collapse in front of them.

28th August, 1884

There is definitely something in the hold. I cannot name it but it is there. I am anxious. Boys can see it on my face. Go less out of my cabin. For their own good.

(It appears that the fear has manifestly moved from the hold to take hold of Mr. Redman. It perhaps represents a shift of oppression away from the boys. Or at least, some terror has shifted its load and fallen upon John Redman. The hulk appears as a nightmare weighing on the brains of the living.)

30th August, 1884

Stay awake listening. Cannot sleep. Hear some boys cry out, for the first time. Did not know they did this. Cry myself about this. Still hear ship groaning. Cannot stand it.

21st September, 1884

Lifeless. Stay inside all day. Think about my children. Wife. What are they doing? Do they miss me? Am too tired to think through this.

(Mr. Redman is about to have a bad dream. I warn you, dear reader, that this man has lost his mind.)

27th September, 1884

Terrible dream last night. Feel the need now to get it down. It was dinner time. I had roused myself from my cabin. Told myself off again for becoming disorganised in my habits. On deck with boys. They move around me as if I were invisible. They have plates in their hands. One boy is sitting by himself. Squatting actually, against some rope on deck. He's holding his plate in one hand and eating with the other. And looking around. There is not much talk at this time. It is very orderly. Unhappy. Solemn. As if they are waiting for something terrible to be announced. The death of someone loved, perhaps. I think to myself that these boys are wounded. And then I can see a dozen wounds in front of me. That drip and ache. It is hideous to admit it, but I put my hand inside a boy.

37

I feel the pain. Touch the walls of his cavity. I think I feel the contours of destitution and poverty. It feels like blood and old mutton. Then I part the tissue. Then I'm looking down into a room. I see toys. I see empty bottles. I see an old armchair and behind it a man is touching a small boy. I am staring at the scene of a man touching a small boy. I do not want to do this. I am unable to tear my eyes away. The man turns around and looks at me. I see his animal teeth. I see his insect wings. They're stretching out. He's going to harm another boy. He's going to harm one thousand times. I'm yelling out 'I want a doctor on board! I want a physic surgeon!'

No answer.

I look out to sea, at the horizon and it has become queer. It is tipping over. There were a tidal wave sitting on the horizon. It has gone all perpendicular.

And that's when I start to vomit. And that was when I awoke. Exhausted. Very anxious. Feeling that all this is coming to a close.

(It was soon after this time that Mr. Redman resigned from the hulk. I do not know if it were the scheme of the Way Commission to undermine him or if, as it seems from the journal, he was becoming somewhat unhinged, or if it were a combination of the two. I have perhaps not been fair to Mr. Redman. But I have been, I believe, faithful to his desire for an analytical narrative. Be that as it may, the journal was to be only the beginning of my inexorable return to the hulk *Fitzjames*.)

THE DOCUMENTS OF THE TEACHER, ALFRED WEIPPERT, AS CONFISCATED BY SUPERINTENDENT JOHN REDMAN

Sept. 1884

Sunday. Caught the train to Largs Bay. Early evening. Made my way to the end of the jetty. Met by Mr. Jefferson, ship's carpenter. Rowed to hulk by boys manning oars. Boys rowed well. Went aboard the hulk at 5.30 pm. Dead calm. Reported myself to acting superintendent (Mr. Thompson) at the gangway. Stated my name and was met warmly. Taken on tour by Mr. Thompson. Visited boys, who were then engaged between decks reading, drawing, playing draughts. Perfect order was being maintained. Mr. Thompson introduced me. Boys seem well mannered enough. Hope they are ready for me. Mr. Thompson tells me the boys are classified into three divisions according to their good conduct. First and second division have privileges in rank, diet and work over the rest. As it was tea-time they were mustered in classes and marched to separate tables. Asked Mr. Thompson what they had for tea. Was told the staple food was a piece of bread and an allowance of treacle. The tea was without milk and sugar. These items having run short for a week past. As one lad passed me I asked him (taking the liberty to do so) I asked him if he had enough to eat. His reply was what might have been expected: 'some do, some don't. You see some boys want more than what others do.' Inspected dormitory. Clean and roomy though somewhat redolent of chloride of lime. Visited boot and shoe workshop. 'Sweat shop' thought I. Went through the rest of the ship: superintendent's office; office; cook's department and private room. Finally led to school room and library. Mr. Thompson informs me that the boy's behaviour is generally good. Stated as proof that for months past the dark-cell had been unused.

Nov. 1884

Notes for myself re. reading these boys' spirit

1. These boys are too used to being read as being bad.

2. To read with hostility is to befriend the power of ignorance. It is to move the eyes and focus the gaze without a taking in, without a movement towards an emotional engagement. It is an inability to move the spirit, to become stuck and fixed without hope, and confused, and fearful, thus to be surrounded by that which threatens sense making, to be surrounded by a lack of sentence structure, to see before one's eye's an inaccessible realm of meaning making, an impossible heap of rubbish, an impossible cache of gold.

3. Reading goes forth from object to subject, ebbing in and out between these two, and so it is that the body that reads becomes the body being read, becomes the actual appearance of reading itself. Reading becomes stuck and immovable at the manifestation and stench of a certain appearance. The appearance which cannot be accommodated, that which must be transformed from a condition of unknowing towards clarity and safety.

4. Reading adversely, it is in this manner of composition that ignorance and fear make their appearance.

5. Being read in stillness, surrounded by nothing, composed in fresh air, placed together quietly, word upon word, is the life that takes place despite us, it is the ever present flow and purge of language, surrounding still being like

a halo, dependent upon the body, and upon the actions of the body, to not be still, to read this flow as if it were the life blood of identity, rather than the ephemera of community, the appearance of another's written composition, the reading of a thousand million other departed souls.

6. Reading still, a still reading, it is without activity, it has no identity, it is partaking of the next world within our own.

7. It is here at the moment of reading that the boy appears. It is at that moment that he is almost set free from the dark shadow, from the strangulation and the night.

8. At the birth of the world, at the beginning of man, at the opening of God's play, there at that moment when the world took shape, there upon the dead plains and lunar valleys, appeared reading.

10. It is to this singular fact, to the reading of a boy, and the appearance of reading, that all who teach must bow down and obey.

I have begun to bring certain boys into my confidence, in a way that they feel able to express themselves and their feelings concerning their life here. I want to understand these boys and feel they could benefit from articulating themselves within an intimate environment. I have begun private writing sessions with certain boys. In particular Boy 3, the Spanish fellow, Cyril, Fook and the Minali boy. I encourage them to express, without constraint, their inner selves. My desire is to get out of the boy what impedes their understanding of themselves and their situation. I should like these sessions to contain the recollections of childhood. I should like it to contain those things that resonate still, that they return to, without cause, as if taken by surprise. These places, they seem to have a power that lingers even in an actual object. A small toy, bad weather, the balcony of a poor dwelling. I want him to recall that experience which has departed, which left for other parts, and has not returned. It is in the writing of their selfhood, within an environment of pastoral care and guidance, an intimate environment where they may peal back the layers of self imposed restraint, it is in that environment that their better selves may find a home.

Have befriended Mr. Jefferson. Late at night he taps at my door and offers me a tour of the hold. On our journey we passed over the great bed of silt which had been placed amidships as ballast. Proceeded to a spot indicated by Mr. Jefferson on the bluff of the starboard bow. Examined the place. Water was running in as fast as it would from a 2-inch tap. Mr. Jefferson took out his knife to try the soundness of the timbers. The blade went straight through the wood, showing it to be thoroughly rotten. As the vessel rolled and lurched the timbers creaked dolefully. The situation seemed rather dismal. Returned to my cabin. Thought about the boys.

Herb Dolan is a troubled boy. Sent down for rape. Aged 12. Cannot take on any lesson. Seems paralysed by idiocy. Ask him to work, like the other boys. Responds by biting fingers. Hard. Puts whole fist in his mouth and bites down. Cannot spell the simple words 'tea', 'sugar', 'once' or 'window'. Holds himself as well. With the other hand. Clutches his genitals. Stamps his feet on the floor. When set a writing task he fills his book with scribble. Will frequently piss himself. Wild looking boy. Cannot get any good from him. Have asked for transfer out of hulk. Disturbs other boys. Talks incessantly of intercourse. Unbearable. Must learn to love him.

Notes re. God's love of learning

1. There is a certain substance in all boys which is wanting to be free and to be ecstatic with a sense of purpose and belonging.

2. This substance is a moral spirit. It is the spirit of His love.

4. Boys can love and smile and quake, yes quake with God's spirit. And I can get that quaking. Arouse it with the right words. The right words will arouse a sense of rightness in the boys.

5.   Love boys. Entwine them in your soul. Feel their sweet energies and guide that sweetness toward the gushing fountain in the sky. Ecstatic thoughts, of being entwined with love and youth.

6.   The sentiments of love can be used for the betterment of boys.

7.   It is the reforming of the self, of developing the self, that I am put here to carry out with love and tenderness and obedience to the long term spiritual emancipation of those boys who are enslaved to a base materiality and who suffer from the pain of too little love.

8.   Boys lack loving tutelage. Lack a loving encouragement for their better self to come forward, and speak, and articulate and appreciate that this is a world which is inhabited with a spiritual presence.

9.   This is a God-infested world, to be short, and these boys will learn it.

Lesson: forgiveness

When it was a cold winter's morning the contents of a large can of cold water were emptied over Walter James' head. Although drenched and shivering, he went in and sat through school. As the day advanced a bright red spot appeared on either cheek, his head burned and the raging fever took him delirious, the fever raged and his pulse continued increasing. A doctor was sent for and because he had a naturally delicate constitution the doctor was full of the gravest anxiety and a severe chill consumed everything. It was with a grieved, anxious expression that the superintendent conducted service that evening. 'I have a few words,' said the superintendent, 'I feel it my painful duty to say to you as you all know someone is now lying at the point of death. And the cause of his death lies at the door of one of you present here. I ask you now to come forward you, the boy who played this mean trick because it is through your instrumentality that Walter James has received his death-blow. So let me impress upon you now this terrible time and how near lies death to each of you, and so I beg of you to examine yourselves, to put to yourselves, each one of you individually, 'am I ready to die?'' Quite overcome, the superintendent sat down, grieved and disappointed, and he looked round and the boys marched into the dark. The next day poor Walter James who was now about to be snatched by the cruel hand of death lay with his hand clasped in mine, and he said 'tell the boys to think of me waiting for them, over there, ask them to come to me soon, and promise me that nothing bad will happen to the boy that did the crime; he only meant it as a joke.' The last words were feeble and barely audible and his hand unclosed its clasp and his eyelids closed, and a convulsive shiver ran through the boy's dead body. The superintendent at once summoned the discovered wretched culprit boy to his cabin, and kindly, but sternly, pointed out to dreadful things. The boy's heart was touched to the core that a dying wish said that he should not be whipped wretched. Carrying out the dying request the superintendent consented to let the boy remain confined and shackled him down below for the remainder of the sentence. From that day he applied himself diligently at his work and soon won esteem. Then one day he sent a petition from himself and the boys for a small memorial window to the remembrance of Walter. It is still to be seen in the starboard side of the hulk. It is the touching representation of Christ suffering on the cross, and the mocking scoffing at him from the shore, while beneath the window are written these words: 'Father, forgive them, for they know not what they do.'

Lesson: spelling

1. One spells the sentence in a manner that is pre-determined. One does not spell a new order, one spells-out an order that is there.

2. One articulates a power that is latent. One gains entry to a certain power by articulating, part by part, a proper order.

The power which one may gain comes out of respect to an in-alienable order; to partake in that, to have power, one must spell-out the way it was ordained, by the higher orders, who want to bestow their power.

3. There is a power that waits.

4. Men gained their power in part by reading out words from letter to letter. They broke down the word of God into component parts, which could not be re-arranged or tampered with. It was then that God appeared to those who heard this, as an infinitely indivisible entity. And the secret to this particular idea, was not that God came from letters, or their pronunciation (all creatures came forth thus) but that God was a unique and singular form of letters. He could not be spelt out any other way. To bring God to bear upon this earth, to make Him present, then there must be proper spelling. And when there is proper spelling then He is present.

5. It is a deformity of the highest order to mis-spell the word of God. It is an abomination to invoke with God's letters, another form of being. The heart of youth is as the page beneath your hand. So one must be sure when writing that the word of God partakes of a proper order, and that it does not dally with those forces of perversion who, knowing the secrets of the power of spelling, wait at the edges of your page.

9. There is a fearfulness gathering at the borders of each word, at the differences between the proper and improper. A certain disintegration looms, where there is disorder and miscegenation, that is where you may find the excluded fellow.

10. There must be an exclusion, a keeping at bay the one, the singular, who belongs some place else, who may not wander into this proper place. That fellow, the one who must belong elsewhere, he too has a home and a duty to which he needs place himself.

11. Fearfulness and disaster creep alongside every line you write. And each boy has this demon looking over him, waiting for the mistake which will invoke the wrath of order. Each boy, at the verge between the pen and paper, is dealing with the difference between disaster and success. He has a chance to make good himself there.

12. On the surface of the page is inscribed the outlines of the fate and character of each and every boy.

∞

Mr. Jefferson wakes me again. Find myself unable to decline his offer of late-night journey. We walk silently through the hulk. He points to weather side of the ship. Suggests I take note how it decays under the effect of the elements. Takes me once again down into the hold. He speaks incessantly about the condition of the boat. How rotten it is. How it will soon sink and kill us all.

'You see here Mr. Weippert, the caulking below the copper is very bad. In several places the oakum is completely decayed, being so bad this ruler here, I can push it through the back of the seam to the copper, leaving only the copper and churram to keep the ship afloat.'

As he spoke he demonstrated that fact with great vigour.

'As you can see here there's water over the ceiling on the port side. Over here, on the starboard side, I've been cutting away some timber to see if there was a leak there too. But I could not make my way in.'

'Why was that?' I asked, as much as to keep some semblance of sanity amid the gloomy darkness. The ship was still lurching. I felt it down amid the darkness, that certain fear, deep within me.

'See all that timber? When she was a quarantine vessel they just tossed it down here without much thought. It's forming a well-consolidated heap, calculated to strain an old ship riding in a seaway. And now it can't be got at. It's too dark in there. Always. The lights I bring don't ever show enough to see at all. Come on here I got to sound the pumps.'

With that I followed him along the dark passage, covered over, as I said before, with silt. We finally emerged, passing by the night-watchman.

Returned to my cabin, disturbed in mind and body.

I look down upon myself, sitting at the table, unable to bring words to bear upon this matter, aware that the matter of a judgment looms, that there may come a knock at the door, and with that the forced entry of a dark presence, who knows all that I have done. He knows all that I have done and takes my hand, and guides it to write. I am forced to write against myself, as though there were some abuse occurring here, of a sordid nature. I am being stripped by a malign hand that travels down inside me. There it brings up words which work against me, there, it has my hand clenched within its own. Now I write that I am bad, that I am doomed, that I have no hope at all. That I will always be so. I become narrow, tiny, slender and almost impossible. I hold on only slightly to my body, which is the target of a hostility, a rage not of my own making.

Lesson: reflection

The superintendent in grating tones said 'see that you make an impression on that boy's back. And have the remaining boys turn up for punishment.' In obedience to the summons the boys on the quarter-deck with awe-stricken faces looked on at the dread scene.

'Very good Mr. Thompson!' said the superintendent, knitting his brows; 'turn out a good cat to your mates.'

'The best I've got in store, sir' replied the gruff man amid profound silence broken by the wind whistling and the sobbing of a wave through the hulk's rigging.

The boy was brought dejected who had been kept under close arrest on the deck, sullen to where stood a grate firmly lashed to the ship by the carpenter. And the mate held lug the dreaded cat-o'-nine-tails in his fist whilst the doctor would report to the superintendent should the boy faint at the terrible punishment during its infliction.

The superintendent, in a loud tone, with reference to the offence of which the boy had been guilty and the sentence folded the paper up, made a signal to the mate who ordered the delinquent to strip off his flannel. And his wrists and ankles were lashed to the grate and the superintendent in firm and grating tones, said 'do your duty.' The mate who held the cat, stepped forward and took position up behind the culprit, who, naked to the waist, cast a furtive glance in dread expectation of the powerful man rolling his sleeve. Displaying a great, hairy, arm, and giving the cato'nine-tails a flourish in the air on the culprit's bare back he began emphatically. The marks became instantly visible of several incisions.

Clearing the cat with his fingers in orthodox fashion with every blow the boy writhed like a serpent. The culprit's back was seamed and lacerated, blue-and-red, and the boys' gaze turned unable any longer.

As the blows struck home the superintendent addressed the boys saying that this cruel punishment and these severe punishments have frequently been the cause of a complete breakdown.

'Know then that a punishment has become a thing of fear of the cat no doubt acting as a deterrent to the evil-disposed.'

At length the two dozen lashings were cast and the boy in a fainting condition was led down below and the superintendent ordered the boys to 'pipe down,' dispersing them below to reflect on the sentence.

∞

Visit the government alienist at the insistence of the hulk doctor. Took myself down to the Destitute Asylum. Grey and miserable day. The heavens echoed the bleak and awful presence of that place. Entered the establishment from Kintore Avenue. Passed what at first I thought was a chapel, but on closer inspection it became clear that the building was in fact a morgue. Saw a coffin. Walked across a dreary sun-less courtyard towards the men's quarters. Inside the stench of filthy flesh and garments. Adjusted my eyes to the dim and dreary light. Began interview with the alienist. Talked about the dead house. The sunless day. The identity of the corpse. Felt ill with this. Something wrong. Bad vapours passed by. The black form. Discussed my mania. The fearful sentences. On leaving he took my hand and shook it firmly. Spoke into my ear, quietly and emphatically.

∞

Mr. Button discovered myself and Mr. Jefferson in the boy's dormitory. Were on our way to the hold again. Stopped by to look at them sleeping. Restful. Calm. Hammocks swaying. Lingered too long. Upset extinguished lamp. Found out by wardsman. He called Mr. Button down. Taken to office for interrogation. He suggested that my position would be reviewed. Has heard some unsavoury rumours. Was going to ignore them, but this matter has changed his mind.

Dreary man. Upstart. Uncultured.

I cannot dis-avow the sickness in me.

What is it that forces my confession?

I am a manifestation of the hand which forces and abuses, that is connected to the night, and to the forces of evil and black desire. Hands come to me at night, and desire to take me to the cell, where children have been turned to bone, where some still hide beneath rock, where the shadows of a tragic disappearance flitter across my eyes.

The candle has blown out. The cell drips blood.

I want judgment to cease its interminable grinding of young flesh. The judgement machine incinerates conscience. It desires the death of conscience. It desires to make all conscience its own so that its terrible grinding can rule this flat sea.

Mr. Jefferson at me again. Enters my quarters. Raving.

'I am of the opinion sir, that the hulk, to make her tight and sea-worthy, ought to be placed on the patent slip, ballast taken out, copper stripped off, all defective planks and fastenings renewed, caulked from keel to covering board, and churammed and sheathed with yellow metal. Probable cost of repairs I make to be three thousand five hundred pounds. I am further of the opinion sir, that she may open out at any moment.'

Told the man that I had other things on my mind at present. Refused to hear more. Told him that I sought redemption.

∞

The night. Dark and a little glimmer from the moon was covered over by clouds. Heard the roar of the sea. Seemed like a mountain. Crossed the deck and walked towards the farthermost part of the hulk. Heard the wheels of the carriages away in the direction of the shore. Found my head running on the story of the dead boy. Seemed to see the gipsy kneeling on the pauper's chest. Cutting his throat with a pocket knife. Said out loud I won't be frightened I won't. There aren't any such things as hosts. Dead boys don't walk about. A hanged wooden figure can't do me harm. I haven't anything to steal.

Coming to the dead boy was the worst part of the way. Feared seeing that ugly form. Tried to fix my mind on a girl whose dress I had torn while we danced. Why was she so angry with me?

Then I saw it quite plain the dark form. It stood out and my heart jumped. Heard a hundred things come up from the grave. Trembled all over. The dark figure stood up and began to move about.

And it saw me and kicked and tugged at his chain. He whined. Oh what I saw was a donkey tied by a chain to the post of the prow. I laughed till my sides split. He lifted up his head and hee-hawed.

Awoke before I felt the ass.

Notes for self improvement

1. I have pain in my own life and I have disaster waiting for me and I have doom casting shade over my wind-swept horizon.

2. I am so vulnerable, fragile and liable to dissipation.

3. I am a third-rate man.

4. I do un-manly work.

5. I am confined, like a woman, with children and their education. I take on this womanly role, for want of something better, for want of some manliness which was never my inclination nor lot it seems.

6. I avert my eyes from most men aboard. We seem to all share a similar shame. To be those who care for boys.

7. I have the lowest rank. The one who deals not with brute force or power, but with soft immaterial and delicate matter, as would a woman with fine lace, which was sewn with invisible threads at night.

Must remember to refuse Mr. Jefferson's advances. I judge myself and find it wanting.

Note: I cannot give in to this sickness (again)

I take myself apart at the moment of judgment. To take the eyes perhaps, from the skull, they do not stare so now. To take away the lips, that do not frown so now. Also, I want to take the hands apart from their arms, to place them down upon the floor. And the brain too, that must come forth from the skull, and sit quietly with those other body parts. There it is then, judgment taken down a peg or two, placed on a tray on the floor. I pick each piece to locate exactly where it is that there is a force. Where the force that holds me lies. Where is it that I am, in this bloody array. I hold and examine each in turn, and imagine myself held in those hands and held in those eyes, which hold nothing now. My corpse holds nothing except an absence. In my imagination those hands and eyes hold me down. The picture of myself being held down keeps me fearful. I am my fearful presence.

∞

Need appears at the beginning of every boy's sentence, and it is at that point where there appears a great need for good writing. For the appearance of a sentence which can re-structure need and transform its poverty to some correct and proper purpose. The painful sentence suffers a paucity of structure, grammar and direction. It lacks words like 'comfort,' 'welcome' and 'love.'

There is a writing which is beyond, which cannot ever be touched and there is a beyond to all writing, the objects of which are never present. Material qualifications, they belong to the material realm and not to good writing.

There is always an identity beyond, or at least there is a presence, in its inessential essentiality, in its formlessness and mystery.

I have put myself where crime has taken place, I place myself there, at the place where the dark shadow falls, where light has fled, where doom strikes, where the last letters fall beneath the sea without sound. The slow strangulation of the blood and of the breath, the inability to communicate and to send a message, it is so isolating, this condition of being adrift. This loneliness that is so complete, that has beginnings but no way of ending or completion.

My mouth. The sentence.

LETTER FROM THE RUNAWAY, JOHN REID, TO THE TEACHER ALFRED WEIPPERT

Dear Sir

I think you should know this story why boys run away or get caught up in crime This is a good thing to have in your book for people to learn This then is the story of why I escaped from the hulk. I hope that you will remember this when you teach it was written down but it is true nonetheless and I can imagine you can improve on it as I was not able to It might seem tall but it is not and you will know that this is how boys lived their life and that we want to be happy that's all. So will you read it and use it as part of the hulk histories because this story is a part of that time Did you need any other stories I have them too and it will be a mutual advantage perhaps if you ask me for them I have many stories for you about boys at the time I was close to them and how we were living Tell me if I am interesting you in what I am writing

I am Sir
Yours truly
John Reid

I had been a boy who got into trouble I was first at the Industrial School for I can't remember what. I got away from there as often as I could I said I shouldn't have been locked up for not liking school that's why I got sent to the hulk originally for absconding from the Industrial School then I was licensed to Mr. Collins in mount Bryan and it was a terrible hard lot and it was dry country with sheep and I was treated bad and buggered I got returned for misconduct Now that I remember it that was the second time after I was sent to a farmer at Second Valley but I was returned for misconduct from there too. Then about when I was about 14 I and another boy it was John Ramage who is not good at all we absconded from the hulk together and we both got caught and the local magistrate who is a sodomite he ordered us to be whipped and we were Ramage got 18 and I only got 12. Then we went back to the hulk after we were whipped I was having a bad time of it and so I went over again.

When I was about 15 I absconded and they never found me as you already know.

On the hulk *Fitzjames* I put both my hands on the shoulders of my mother who had come to the hulk for one of the visits the superintendent gave I loved my mother and she smiled through tears but why was it especially heavy upon her at that moment? There was things troubled Mrs Reid and whitened her hair.

  'Is it Vincent ?' I said.

  'Oh John ! If your brother would only come home for his birthday!'

  'Oh he'll come back' I said 'Why are you troubled?'

  'Hark!' said Mrs Reid. The sound of bells came full and clear over the sea

  'They rang like that the night he left us '

  'Oh! John ' my mother said 'that was two years ago!'

She sank down and she covered her face and she wept freely.

  'Don't fret my mother ' I said I kissed her

My mother said 'you are a good boy' and she cried all the way home to her house.

It was an amazing thing but that same day there was a letter come for me and ît was the mate who gave ît to me saying 'this is from your brother Vincent' I opened ît and I could hardly believe ît but I managed alright and ît went like this.

Dear John I want you to meet me to-night at half-past twelve on the swamp I will tell you why I must see you at that time and at that place when you come. If you tell anybody a word about this letter or bring anybody with you won't find me there You must come by yourself and without anybody knowing if you ever want me to come home again You will be surprised but you will understand ît when you get there. Hoping to see you down by the old gate at half-past twelve tonight

I am
Your affectionate brother
Vincent Reid

This is not my handwriting as you will see. I have hurt my finger and can't write and a friend has written me If you wish me to meet you there and go home with you not a word of this to anybody.

So that is why I absconded because I was needed desperately by my trusted brother who was in trouble and you know how I did ît now I will repeat what happened.

It was the darkest night with the stillness in the oppressive swamp I was feeling the loneliness and the strangeness of the escape in the 'witching hour of night' I however was not daunted now that I had made up my mind. Now and again the breeze went sobbing over the hill-top and ever and anon the hoarse and solemn roar of the distant sea came swelling through the darkness Down into a valley now and across a slight wooden bridge spanning a brook whose swollen waters rumbled and gurgled as if catching the far-off thunder of the sea Another narrow field and I had reached what was perhaps the most formidable part of my journey — a narrow lane or rather footpath through a coppice. Many a time had I been in the middle of a field in the darkness with my mother exploring mossy dells following her before out at midnight but certainly never had I seen inside the course of the streamlets that bubbled through it or sat on some fallen tree as now and watched the gambols of fire I had crept stealthily down the back staircase of rabbits across the open spaces amid their houses had drawn back the somewhat ponderous clustering ferns and the masses of bluebells. Alas! How strange the place looked and what clouds were scudding! As if there was bolts and bars on the outer door and I stood beneath it on a spot in the midnight stars Across clear frosty light that was teeming with pleasant memories How still and solemn those stars looked at the dead hour.

And low on fully the old door creaked out I pushed open the creaky old gate and hinges As the boy stepped into the wood how weird and strange and nervous it was it must be confessed. That narrow path I knew not echoed by old winter church clocks It then began to boom out the midnight hour! The night had never known it was the dead of night it was shrouded in a winding-sheet of mist.

I was on the point of emergence and was beginning to congratulate myself that my brother must be now within a very short distance when clear above the rustle of the breeze came a short sharp whistle and the whistle I had heard a signal to me over at the quarry and the next minute a tall obscure figure moved into the pathway. For a moment the boy's heart seemed to stand still It could be Vincent who had come to me my throat and lips were terribly dry and I stood for a moment as if paralysed But it occurred to me this might be one of my brother's stealing companions who was not more than a gunshot from where I stood. I put a bold-front on and because it may be only an honest wayfarer But my knees shook an instant after I had come up fairly in front of the first burly form a second one hove in sight I felt some serious mischief in my hand.

I met two rough men in the dark and they took hold of me roughly and I was afraid of them. I said what do you want and they said they wanted me but I didn't know what they were about I said I wanted my brother and if they knew about him They said they was sent by him and I had to do what they said. They were mean and you can see that I would be afraid as it was dark in the swamp And they wanted me to steal and rob my family for them But I was not about to do that because I wanted to get away from that life and because the hulk was waiting for me again you see I did not want to be on the hulk and I wanted to be with my brother.

Swift as a crushing thunderbolt and a flash of lightning I knew the poor lad that I had been made the cruel victim of a hoax there would be no returning my brother no restoration of my mother's peace and happiness and then I would be back at the hulk for no good at all. I had braved the peril of the swamp and the bitter cold and I had come with a heart full of love for the wanderer and beating high with the hope of bringing him home and you see now it appeared that the letter from that wanderer was merely heartless bait to get me in the power of ruffians and burglars!

I am a manly boy but for one moment I looked upon the man with a look of pale and speechless agony and then burst into tears.

    'Come come!' said one of the strangers 'there's no need for any o' that You needn't be afraid. You have only got to —'

    'Afraid!' blazed out the boy with passionate vehemence 'I am not crying because I am afraid Don't you think it!'

    'Well what then?' growled the fellow.

    'Why — I thought my brother Vincent had —'

I could get no further and again put an arm across my face and cried tears bitterly.

    'Look here!' said one of the men shaking me by the shoulder and speaking in a rough threatening tone 'we've no time for this Tell us what we want to know and then you can blubber us long as you like.'

'D'ye think I'm going to help you rob my uncle and my mother?' broke out the young captive drawing himself up and quivering with desperate defiance in the fibre of my body

The two men exchanged glances villains they were impressed by my valorous bearings who had taken whippings before and was not scared of no man. The look they gave each other would have said as much if the twinkling stars had thrown more light on the black night

'Very well ' said the man 'we have only to go and walk in by the door and get the plate whether you tell us where it is or not But unless we know just where to drop on it it'll take us some time to rummage and if anybody was to interfere with us while we are at it they night get hurt. D'ye see? You wouldn't like your uncle or your mother to get a crack with a crowbar would you? If we know just where 'tis we can go and get it and have done with it and nobody's be hurt and you can go as soon as you like in the morn'.

I had a bad choice and I did not want to hurt my mother and I did not want them to be hurting her so you see this is how boys get into trouble They have no choices but are made to be bad and then they get sent away.

'Now then ' said the criminal fellow who was an escaped man too giving a rough shake to the shoulder he held 'What's it to be? Are you going to tell us?'

I clenched my fist drew up and looking straight into what of the criminal face could be seen I said 'kill me'

'Now look here young man' said the fellow who gripped me viciously as he spoke 'we don't mean to stand no nonsense and we've got no time to spare. You know what this is I dare say?' he continued and he cocked a pistol in my mouth 'I'll give you about fuck nothing seconds to think about it and if you don't do as we wants you then I'll blow your brains out'.

I visibly shrank from the terrible thing. It was another thing that made me have no choice But I thought I did in that I could die so you see that is another good choice for boys eh sir? You can die or be part of crime that's what. And I escaped to do good and save my brother but wherever I goes I has got pain and torment and that is how I see it too there is nowhere for like us to go who make the choices and they kill us or send us out to crime and then onto a ship that is like the dead night with no stars shining in it.

'I shall not think about it' I said 'I am not going to help you rob my uncle. If you murder me you must' the man scowled upon me and levelled the weapon at my eye I shrank back again and threw up my arm as if to shield my face but never a word could my torturer wrest from me. This was very awkward They would have liked to have shot me because I was a criminal boy any way and not good even as a dog But they did not and the men held a brief consultation in whispers and then one of them said 'you'll be sorry for this before long my fine fellow ' he growled and as he spoke he stroked me the face of the boy who stood breathless and trembling at the edge of the precipice.

You may think that the boys were used to violent things like this but we weren't. I knew some of those boys and they were not there because they were violent There was boys who were there because all they did was steal something useless or some small thing or something to eat and they might be uncontrollable and why was that? Those boys they would play around and wouldn't you too? What's natural ways for boys is scary and they jump on us for it they think boys are doing something wrong when you know they're hanging around flexing their muscle Why is it that they're so hard on us? We're not as destructive as they think They think we're a lot worse than we are You know usually the victims of violence are boys They're likely more to be victims than the other way round.

'Now I'll tell ye what we're going to do' said the criminal man 'and then you can think about it.'

'My mate's gone off to fetch some more of 'em and if you don't out with what we want we're going to pitch you over the cliff into the sea.'

A bitter cry of anguish broke from the parched and ashy lips of the young captive and I clasped my hands upwards in the dark night.

'I shouldn't think God would let you do that' I said.

'You wouldn't think God let poor men starve but he do though' ejaculated the criminal.

'If I were a man like you I'd rather starve ten times over than serve a poor little chap like this.'

Tears again relieved my heart hotly They streamed down from beneath my bandage and my sobs which I would have repressed if I could perhaps softened the rugged and brutal nature of the smuggler Then he spoke somewhat less harshly persuading me that all I had to do was to comply with the demand made upon me and I needn't be afraid. I would be quite safe if I would tell them where to find some valuables.

'I won't! I won't! I won't!' again I broke out with the fiercest yell 'What sort of a boy would I be to go home and find my uncle and my mother away and murdered and know that I had helped to do it! I never will. Even if God lets you throw me into the rocks I tell you I won't do it!'

As if the incident had been part of a dream being told that I would have to die soon or tell it was then all was oblivion till I opened my eyes and found someone bending over me.

'John John old boy! Don't be afraid it's Vincent.'

In an instant us two locked in a fond and fervent embrace.

'Are they going to do it Vincent ?' I asked in a hoarse whisper.

'To do what John?'

'To rob our house?'

'The villains! The dastardly villains!' broke out my brother.

'Are they going to kill me?' I whispered.

'I don't know ' answered Vincent. 'I don't know what they are about.'

'Oh Vincent my dear old Vincent did you send that letter to me? And what did you send it for? Did you really mean that perhaps you would come home?'

'What letter John ?'

'A man brought me a letter' said me sobbing on my brother's shoulder. 'The letter asked me to meet you in the swamp at half-past twelve tonight and it said perhaps if I did you would go home with me.'

Vincent groaned pressing both his hands to his forehead. 'Oh John old boy! I wish I had never come away from home I didn't think they were villains What did they do it for?'

One of the men who stood near with a face partially concealed by masks said to me 'don't you know anything about your brother?'

'Go back again Vincent' said me rising to my elbow and speaking with all the eagerness of my soul 'go back again to mother Oh wouldn't we have a birthday! Go Vincent ! Do!'

Vincent Reid shook his head sadly. 'Mother'd be ashamed of me.'

'Why Vincent our dear old mother ashamed of you! Why she's always praying that you may come back and cries about you and her hair's all turned grey Vincent and only last night when the bells were ringing they put her in mind of you and when I looked up she was crying ready to break her heart and she said 'oh if Vincent would only come home to my birthday!' Come on Vincent why she'll be half frantic with joy!'

Vincent listened to this impassioned outpouring with a face full of amazement and then tears stole down his keen sin-marked visage.

'I thought my mother would have given me up John. God bless her old boy! But I can't go back John'

'Why not Vincent ?'

The wanderer shook his head.

'I'm too much mixed up with 'em ' he said. 'I never meant to be John I didn't mean to be as bad as I have been but when you begin to go bad you never know when you're going to stop You should know about that. I thought it was only a bit of stealing they were up to and some folks think there isn't so much harm in stealing But they're a bad lot John and now I'm one of them I can't break from 'em now. They'd shoot me if I did.'

'Let 'em shoot' said me stoutly I'd rather they should shoot me fifty times than be one of them.'

The opinions of most of the company as expressed in whispers and muttered curses was that it was no use going any further and one or two began discussing the expediency of killing me

It was then that Vincent at last spoke with my true heart:

'I am dumbfounded both at the terrible display of villainy on the part of you men and at the splendid boy whom I had been wont to think of as a thug I see the craft and wickedness of the scheme and well how the threats to shoot you John and to fling you down the rocks have been made. John you have withstood all their violence! Thrice this night you have faced death rather than do a single act of wrong to the good old man who is father to us both and to mother whose hair has turned grey with our waywardness and wickedness I know my conduct is so wretchedly ignoble and degraded so utterly contemptible and unworthy.'

And a sensation flashed through my mind with startling force. If these villains should really rob my uncle and I were apprehended who would believe me though I should swear that I knew nothing about it? I had been reckless and wild but I was not wholly hardened and I stood aghast at the thought of appearing as an accomplice in so heartless a crime-plundering the old gentleman and mother.

'John' said my brother 'you're the noblest and best and bravest boy I know I don't a bit deserve what you've gone through for me. Forgive me.'

'Vincent I am here to set you free So I say to you and to your companions exchange me for him. Let Vincent go and I will tell you all!'

It was an incredible turn of events but that is what happened.

Vincent went home to my mother and uncle and they were all weeping and he said 'aye mother a bad fellow can come good. It was the bravery of John who set me free and helped me see how wrong I was.'

But for me I could never go home and I was always on the run from my home and is it justice that such a boy should have suffering like that?

The robbers did not get to my house and take the possessions because I foiled them at the last moment. That is what sort of boy I was.

That is the end of the story of John Reid who was an inmate of the hulk who was not a bad boy at all and who should be remembered as I had told this story as one like all the other boys who suffered because they had no choice.

And because there are bad men all around us.

THE SCRAPBOOK OF ALFRED WEIPPERT, AS DISCOVERED BY THE AUTHOR AT THE HOME OF JAMES BURNS

I should like the book to contain the recollections of a childhood. I should like it to contain those things that resonate still, that we return to, without cause, as if taken by surprise. These places, they seem to have a power that lingers even in an actual object. A small toy, bad weather, the balcony of a poor dwelling. Feeling there once was an experience, which has departed, which left for other parts, and has not returned.

I'm following the aimless flow of memory. I follow it to its final point, to where it flows forth inside another body, to its mouth, where waves of fresh and salt water mix. It is at that point where sharks lurk and pace. I have seen the sky darken at the mouth of the river and I have seen the mists that hide the water spirits, and I have invoked, abused and conversed with these spirits, and I say that amid that drift there is power and memory.

I think the thing I dream of is getting back on the outside world, having your freedom, go to school like a normal person, hang out with your friends, see who you want, within reason, and just get on with your life and show everyone else that you are not a loser. Because that's pretty much how the workers treat you in here, like you're a loser. You're nothing, we're here to control you, you do as we say, and you'll get somewhere.

This place doesn't teach you discipline, just gives you somewhere to stay while you do your sentence. This is just somewhere where you live. It doesn't teach you nothing. Only way you are going to change is if you like change by yourself. You need like an army camp or something. Doing all the discipline stuff like learning how to take orders and that. And do as you're told and things like that. And here they don't treat us like young adults, they treat us like little kids. Once you are naughty you have to go to bed at 7 o'clock. If you are in a boot camp and you're naughty you have to do push-ups. You'd have to show respect to the officer. Here you don't really. You have to show respect but it's just not like a boot camp.

It's alright here, it just doesn't teach you nothing.

I was 13 years old and one day I just went and broke into the school.

I just felt like breaking into the school. And then I just got busted doing that. And I got let off easy.

And from then on I just kept going and going.

After mum started going out with my brother's and sister's dad I started seeing my real dad. I didn't see my dad for a while and then I started seeing my dad again, when I was about 10 or 11. That made a difference. I had like a father figure. And that was important.

My dad comes and visits me every now and then.

Sometimes I feel disgusted with myself because I can't believe I done some of the things I did and inflicted so much pain on my family and on myself as well for only a couple of minutes of pleasure. So sometimes I feel really disappointed, sometimes disgusted in how I was so stupid to lead my life the way I did. And how I could put my parents through that. Making them feel guilty. Thinking what have they done wrong with my up-bringing.

Leaving them with that thought.

When it had nothing to do with them.

It was just a path that I chose at the time.

You come here and you've been taken away from your family and your family's been taken away from you. That's what really matters to me. My family and the one that I love. That's my girlfriend. And it hurts. Everyday of your life in here it hurts. It hurts so much. And you give up your life just to see your family, and just to see your girlfriend not living through hurt. They're hurting out there and I'm hurting in here. If I go out there now that would be the happiest day of my life because I'll be re-united with my family and my girlfriend. People that I love.

It just hurts everyday. It just hurts.

I consider rehabilitation is like a psychological thing.

Like they have to go out and do crime. They have to do crime for the money or they have to do crime for the adrenalin. But I don't have to do crime. I can stop crime whenever I want. I went through a phase where I just did crime for the hell of it. And then I realised that its not benefiting anyone really. Myself, my family or the society. So I just realised that given a push in the right direction that can deter me.

From going back into that same frame of mind.

In the outside world everything's changing. When you are here time stays still. Same thing every day but when you are on the outside things change, things get built, things move, shops move.

Shops get built. Your friends move.

In here its the same every day, time stands still.

I've had heaps of chances. I just keep coming back to crime. It's just fun. Easy to get away with. You can do it when you want. It's always there.

If you want to do something you can always do it.

But I don't want to do crime when I get out. I don't want to come back. Some people don't want to do crime when they get out, some do. Just depends. If you've got a long sentence you've got time to think about it.

Just think. You could be on the outside going to parties and shit like that.

What I can see is that they're trying to help people get in touch with their feelings and their thoughts, and make them connect up with what they're actually doing. Like with their physical being. Trying to influence us residents to sort of think about what we're doing. And if we were going to go out and get back into crime, think about it first. Whether it's right or wrong. Whether we should do it or whether we shouldn't. What's going to be good for us. What's going to be good for people around us. That's what they're trying to do. Just help us be better within ourselves. Not to actually change us. Just be better within ourselves. That's what I can see anyhow.

There's nothing to break the boredom and break the routine.

When you're asleep they've got checks every fifteen minutes. If you've just gone to sleep the lights gone off the light comes on you, wakes you up again. Takes you a while to get back to sleep. It makes me feel pissed off. Get sick of it after a while. Sick of the same old routine. There's nothing to break the boredom and break the routine.

Nothing you really can do.

There's no purpose to us being in here at all. I mean the only thing the kids in here want to do is to keep on escaping. Get their freedom back, because half of them are in here for the same reason as me.

You have to do what they say whether it's right or wrong.

There's no way to get through to them that what you are doing was nothing wrong.

The rules that these guys got here, and the way that we live on the outside — the way most of us live on the outside — sometimes we don't even know we're breaking the rules. Because it's just natural for us to do things like that. If someone wants to fight, for most of us there's no way in the world that we'll say no, I don't want to fight you, let's talk about it. We'll get up and we'll fight straight out. And we'll accept the consequences later. Or we won't even think about the consequences.

They want to go and arrest people, lock them up, and they are not going to teach them anything, all you are going to learn is how to be more of a criminal. Better ways to do things. It's ridiculous. Why not with all that money they spend throwing people in gaol try and find out the problem and fix it? It's like a bad dog, He keeps urinating on your carpet so you are just going to chuck him in the room and lock him up, that's going to teach him not to urinate on the carpet? You got to get to the source and you got to find out, well he's doing it because of this and I've got to teach him.

That's one thing the government is not willing to do.

You don't need to do anything for anybody or make anyone happy. You do it for yourself. And now I'm going to school. Make my parents proud of me. That's the way I want it. I want my parents to be proud of me. That's all I want now. Because my dad's resented me from the first time I ever did crime. But now that I'm in lock-up he knows that I've learnt a lesson. He comes and sees me two times a week. That's all we get here, two visits a week. And he sees me two times a week. And he talks to me normally. Like father and son. Like I always wanted.

He loves me, and he shows that he cares. And he tells me that he loves me. And when I get out I'll mow the lawn for him. Anything that he tells me to do. I'll do it for him.

Because out there I took every day for granted.

And ever since I come here...everyday is like...I just want one day outside, with everyone else, in the community, just to walk on the road. I'll give up anything just for that.

I go crazy if I don't have my freedom and that's what it's like, I'm starting to go crazy.

That's what I'm thinking about all the time.

You look outside your window during the night, you see the stars and you think I wish I was out there, you know, not in here.

There is a remembering of the forlorn and the lonely, and it finds an ally in the remembering and reading which sets itself adrift from all that is fixed and anchored. It is cast out from the garden of identity, certainty and peace of mind.

Astounding things are at the end of the world, at the foreshore where I can see the absence and quietude that comes at the end of the sentence.

Although I want to kill, although I want to destroy, although all this is written and recorded I am haunted by this remanent thought, which to be truthful is but a string of words, hung round my neck, and lowering me, as garlic would an undead corpse, which I am not, and refuse to be.

I am not undead and refuse to be so, although the sentence, that weighs so heavily, that there was something left behind, there is something in this, some thing that will not let me be.

CONCLUSION

I live in a small house in the woods. I collect fire wood at night.
I wake in the morning and say my prayers. I pray to God to
make me a good person. To help me become a good person.
I take a little exercise. I drink water. I light a fire. I cook oats
and eat them with milk and honey. I look out the window. I see
the sun shining on a grass field in Russia. I see the wind blowing
through a grass field in Russia. My clock chimes. I hear a
mouse noise. I open my book. I try to open the book but it
won't come. Why do pages stick together? Sometimes I have
dreams where I can't open my eyes. Sometimes they are stuck
together too.

I put the book down. There's nowhere to go. I'm empty again.
I stand still in the wooden room. Nothing happens. The birds
sing, the wind blows, but not for me, when nothing happens.
The world is spinning, the floor is beneath my feet, but not
for me. All of creation lives without me.

Sometimes I walk outside so that I can walk outside. I open
the door. I love that door. Outside. Nothing. I have no
motivation. I walk even though I have no motivation. Through
the forest, and the tress, and the undergrowth, where there is
a spider, and a squirrel, and a small man who cries out for
help. I don't want to believe that. I am trying to be good. I want
calm. I walk then.

In the woods there is a figure. He walks towards me. He offers

me his hand. We walk to a creek. He takes off his clothes.
He walks into the water. He asks me to come too. I take off
my clothes and go in. We dive down to the bottom and there,
at the very bottom, is a cave. We go down inside it. We emerge
onto dry rock. In the cave is a small chapel. There is incense
burning and there are columns of stone. Another man
emerges from the temple. He has a knife. He comes closer
to me. The first man pins my arms back. The second man has
my throat in his hands. They cut my throat. They put me on
the ground. I'm holding my throat. Blood comes out. I let
the blood come out. I let the blood flow down and the two
men watch. I am being drained. The first man collects my
blood in a bowl. The second man puts robes around me.
He puts flowers on my head. He guides me to a chair, where
I sit. The first man takes the bowl of blood and places it in
the temple. He drinks some blood. The second man binds
my wound. I rest. And sleep. I wake up in my house. It is
morning. It is raining. I'm alright.

I live in desert in a small house built of sticks. I sleep during
the day and look for food when it's cool. I catch birds that are
red and black. I paint their blood onto my skin. I put ash on
my skin. I dance on the sand. I worry about strangers.

I'm hungry so I walk and I walk and I walk. On the horizon is
a moon. I see myself from behind walking towards the moon.
As a black silhouette, surrounded by orange fire. I have a
stick, and, I fear to say, a boomerang. I am walking towards
the moon and I walk. I'm moving along now higher in the sky
as if I were departing like a kite or a dead man. I'm departing
on a perpendicular angle away from the man who has
continued onwards. He throws his spear at me vengefully now
I'm hit and fall. I can see my actual body now. White and with
a spear in my torso collapsed on the sand. Now the man is
cradling my head he's blowing a mouthful of saliva and sand
in my ear as if to bring me back to life. That is the end. He's
holding my head in his hands. I'm alive.

It is summer, it is spring. Long grass with corn flowers. I stand up.

Walk through the field. Walk towards the gate. Climb on the gate. Stand on the top of the gate. I call out for something. I call out for someone. I'm not doing anything. The wind's blowing the field. What's happening is outside. What's important here is not me. I'm still. Balancing on the fence. I see myself falling. I see myself holding my hands in front of my mouth as if blocking a scream. I'm not screaming. I'm balancing. It's quiet. I'm in the sun. It's everywhere and especially in the song of a bird that I hear coming from the edge of the forest. Why does this move me? The important thing is where I am. It is summer, it is spring. Why is this so moving, invisible and timeless? Not as in forever and ever. Just not inside time.

I have to die because I have to die. Because I am angry. Because my heart is black. Because I will never have any money. I have to die because I can't have money. I have to die because I should be dead. I should be dead because I am dead. I should be dead because I am dead. What does it matter that I am alive? I should be dead because when you look at me you can see that I am useless and worthless and genuinely repulsive. I am totally ridiculous. I have to die because I am dead.

I am not dead.

Someone who thinks they are dead said that.

Feels sad about all of the dead people. Feels sad about the dead people who died a long time ago and who are all dead.

2003

I am dead because I am dead.

Between 1883 and 1884.

Still waves. No wind. Nothing.

The introduction by the author, and the conclusion, explaining in his own terms, the motivation for his research and the style and approach of his writing, represent the results of the author's research.

REFERENCES

Boys Own Annual. London, Leisure Hour Office. Volume III (1880-81) and Volume IX (1886-7)

Dickey, Brian. *Rations, Residences, Resources: A History of Social Welfare in South Australia Since 1836*. Adelaide: Wakefield Press, 1986

Hunter, Ian. 'Four Anxieties about English'. *Southern Review* 29.1 (1996): 4-18

Kerr, Heather. 'Fictocritical Empathy and the Work of Mourning' (Forthcoming Cultural Studies Review, 2003)

King, Noel. 'My Life Without Steve: Postmodernism, Ficto-Criticism, and the Paraliterary'. *Southern Review* 27.3 (1994): 261-275

Nettelbeck, Amanda. 'Notes Towards an Introduction'. *The Space Between: Australian Women Writing Fictocriticism*. Ed. Heather Kerr and Amanda Nettelbeck. Nedlands, Western Australia: University of Western Australia Press, 1998: 1-17

Register of Admissions to the Reformatory Hulk Fitzjames. n.d. [unpublished]

Second and Final Report of Commission Appointed to Report on the Destitute Act, 1881; Together with Minutes of Proceedings, Evidence, and Appendices. Adelaide: Government Printer, 1885

SAPP [South Australia, Parliamentary Papers] (39) 1887 p3

Ulmer, Gregory L. 'Mystory: The Law of Idiom in Applied Grammatology'. *The Future of Literary Theory*. New York: Routledge, 1989: 304-323